HANDBOOK

FOR

LONDON COLLEGE OF MUSIC

GRADE FOUR EXAMINATION

IN

CLASSICAL GUITAR PLAYING

General Editor: Tony Skinner

A CIP record for this publication is available from the British Library
ISBN: 1-898466-24-6

Published in Great Britain by

Registry House, Churchill Mews, Dennett Rd, Croydon, Surrey CR03JH

Printed and bound in Great Britain by Redwood Books, Trowbridge, Wiltshire

INTRODUCTION

This publication is part of a progressive series of ten handbooks, primarily intended for candidates considering taking the London College Of Music Step or Grade examinations in classical guitar playing. However, given each handbook's wide content of musical repertoire, and associated educational material, the series provides a solid foundation of musical education for any classical guitar student – whether intending to take an examination or not. Although the handbooks can be used for independent study, they are ideally intended as a supplement to individual or group tuition, and are not designed to replace the need for tuition from an experienced tutor.

An examination entry form is provided at the rear of each handbook. This is the only valid entry form for the London College Of Music classical guitar examinations. Please note that if it is detached and lost, it will not be replaced under any circumstances and the candidate will be required to obtain a replacement handbook to obtain another entry form.

Signs, symbols and abbreviations used in the handbooks

Right-hand fingering is normally shown on the stem side of the notes. *p* = thumb; *i* = index; *m* = middle; *a* = third.

Left-hand fingering is given in numbers 1,2,3,4, normally to the left side of the note head. 0 indicates an open string.

String numbers are given in a circle normally below the note. ⑥ = 6th string.

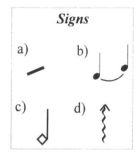

Finger shift is indicated by a small horizontal dash. E.g. 4 - 4 This means that the 4th finger stays on the string but moves to another fret as a *guide finger*. This should not be confused with a *slide* or *glissando* (see example a) where the notes in between the two principal notes are sounded.

Slurs are indicated by a curved line between two notes of differing pitch (see example b).

Full Barrés (covering 5 or 6 strings with the first finger) are shown by a capital B; e.g. BII indicates a barré at the second fret. A dotted line will indicate the duration for which the barré should be held.
Half barrés (covering 2 to 4 strings) are shown like this: ½B

Harmonics are shown with a diamond shaped notehead (see example c). The fret at which they are to be played will be shown above each note; e.g. H7. On the stave they will be placed at the pitch of the string on which they are played, rather than the pitch at which they sound.

Arpeggiated chords (i.e. broken or spread chords) are indicated by a vertical wavy line (see example d).

Editorial information
All performance pieces should be played in full - including all repeats shown. The pieces have been edited specifically for examination use, with all non-required repeat markings omitted. Examination performances must be from the official handbook editions. Standard, or ⑥ = D, tunings have been used for all transcriptions. If preferred, candidates are free to use ③ = F# for lute pieces, or other tunings where appropriate. Tempos, fingering, and dynamic markings are for general guidance only and need not be adhered to rigidly. At higher grades particularly, such markings are often kept to a minimum to allow candidates to display individual interpretation. The omission of editorial dynamic markings does not in any way imply that dynamic variation should be absent from a performance.

Acknowledgements
The Series General Editor acknowledges the help of the many libraries that facilitated access to original manuscripts, source materials and facsimiles. The editor is grateful for the advice and support of all the members of the Registry Of Guitar Tutors 'Classical Guitar Advisory Panel', and is particularly indebted for the expertise and contributions of:

Chaz Hart LRAM, Alan J. Brown LTCL,
Carlos Bonell Hon.RCM, Chris Ackland GRSM LRAM LTCL,
Keith Beniston FLCM GLCM MTC, Gillian Patch MMus LLCM(TD) LGSM LTCL.

SECTION 1 - FINGERBOARD KNOWLEDGE

A maximum of 15 marks may be awarded in this section of the examination.

The examiner will ask you to play *from memory* any of the scales, arpeggios or chords shown on the following pages, as well as those required for previous grades. Refer to the Examination Syllabus or the relevant Handbooks if you are unsure about these requirements.

Scales and arpeggios should be played *ascending and descending*, i.e. from the lowest note to the highest and back again, without a pause and without repeating the top note. *Apoyando* (rest strokes) or *tirando* (free strokes) can be used providing a good tone is produced.

Chords should be played *ascending only*, and sounded string by string, starting with the lowest root note. To achieve a legato (i.e. smooth and over-ringing) sound, the whole chord shape should be placed on the fingerboard before, and kept on during, playing. Chords should *always* be played tirando, i.e. using free strokes.

To allow for flexibility in teaching approaches, the right and left hand fingering suggestions given below are *not* compulsory and alternative systematic fingerings, that are musically effective, will be accepted.

Suggested tempos are for general guidance only. Slightly slower or faster performances will be acceptable, providing that the tempo is maintained evenly throughout.

Overall, the examiner will be listening, and awarding marks, for accuracy, evenness and clarity.

Recommended right hand fingering and tempo		
Scales:	alternating *im* or *ia* or *ma*	96 minim beats per minute
Arpeggios:	*pimaima* (reverse descending)	76 minim beats per minute
Chords:	*p* on all bass strings *ima* on all treble strings	132 minim beats per minute

Melodic Key Study

The Melodic Key Study links the introduction of a new key to the performance of a short melodic theme; from a piece by a well known 'classical music' composer. The purpose is to make the learning of scales relevant to practical music making and therefore memorable, as well providing the opportunity to play music outside the standard guitar repertoire.

The examiner may request you to play any, or all, of the scales within the key study. The examiner may also ask for a performance of the melodic theme. Metronome marking and fingering are for guidance only and need not be rigidly adhered to – providing a good musical performance is produced. The examiner will be listening, and awarding marks, for evidence of melodic phrasing and shaping, as well as for accuracy and clarity. *The Melodic Key Study must be played entirely from memory.*

E Chromatic scale - 2 octaves

D Melodic Minor scale - 2 octaves

A Major scale - 2 octaves

D Major arpeggio - 2 octaves   D Minor arpeggio - 2 octaves

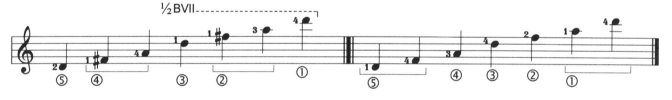

A Minor Barré chord   F# Minor Barré chord

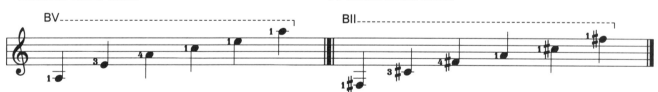

A Dominant 7th Barré chord   B Dominant 7th Barré chord

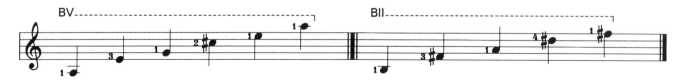

4

Melodic Key Study

Eb Major scale - 2 Octaves

C Harmonic Minor scale - 2 octaves

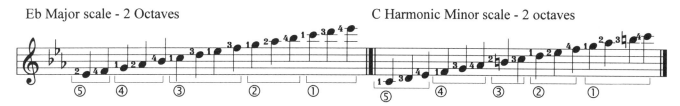

C Melodic Minor scale - 2 octaves

Romance from Eine Kleine Nachtmusik

Wolfgang Amadeus Mozart
(1756 - 1791)

♩ = 84

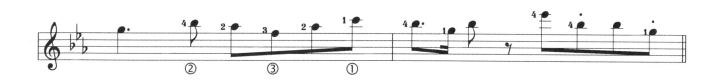

5

SECTION 2 – PERFORMANCE

Candidates should play *one* piece from *each* of the three groups. A maximum of 60 marks may be awarded in this section of the examination - i.e. up to 20 marks for each performance. Fingering and tempo markings are for general guidance only and do not need to be adhered to strictly. All repeat markings should be followed.

PERFORMANCE NOTES

Pavan (Milán): This piece was originally written for the vihuela in the sixteenth century by the Spanish court musician and composer Luis Milán. The *Pavan* should be rather grand and stately in character. The chords in the first three bars should not be snatched or rushed, as they set the tempo for the remainder of the piece.

Lady Laiton's Almain (Dowland): This piece was originally written for the lute by the most renowned lutenist of the period. John Dowland, although born in Ireland, lived in England. He travelled widely in Europe and was appointed as lutenist to the King of Denmark.. The *Almain* should be played at a moderate tempo. Great care needs to be taken with right hand string selection when playing chords such as those in bar two.

Gavotte (De Visée): From a Suite in D Minor, this piece was originally written for the baroque guitar by Robert de Visée – who was employed as the guitar teacher to the King of France. Care should be taken to identify the phrasing. Some appropriate ornamentation could be employed to good effect.

Andantino (Sor): Born in Spain, Fernando Sor also lived in England, Russia and France. He was a well respected and prolific composer – writing over 400 pieces for the guitar. A full range of dynamics should be used to enhance the character of this piece.

Capriccio (Giuliani): Mauro Giuliani was born in Italy and later lived in Austria. He was one of the greatest guitar virtuosos of his day, as well as a profilic composer. This *Capriccio* should be played with a good sense of movement and with the bass voice clearly defined.

Etude (Tárrega): Spanish guitarist Francisco Tárrega is often called 'the father of the modern classical guitar' due to his great influence on technique and repertoire. This study in the key of E Minor is very much in the Romantic vein. The melody is on the first string throughout and should be well defined with a full, but not overpowering, tone. A four fret stretch is required in bar 12 and care should be taken not to release the G bass note before the end of this bar.

Allegretto (Ponce): Mexican composer Manuel Ponce wrote a large number of pieces for the guitar, mainly because of his association with the guitarist Andrés Segovia. This Allegretto should be played at a fairly lively tempo with a well defined sense of rhythm, to bring out the repeated 1&a 2&a rhythmic pattern.

Corsa (Smith Brindle): British born guitarist and composer Reginald Smith Brindle spent many years living in Italy. He has composed over 60 contemporary pieces for the classical guitar. *Corsa* is part of the collection *Ten Simple Preludes*. The piece makes much use of left hand ligados. Notes not slurred within any bar should be allowed to continue sounding together.

Sea Prelude (Hart): British guitarist Chaz Hart is an examiner in guitar playing. He has recorded and composed several works for classical guitar, including a guitar concerto. Sea Prelude involves the repeated use of first finger glissando. The notes in between the two principal notes should be allowed to sound. The dynamic markings should be closely followed to capture the mood of the piece.

Pavan

[Group A]

Luis Milan
(c1500 - 1561)

Lady Laiton's Almain

[Group A]

John Dowland
(1563 - 1626)

Gavotte

[Group A]

Robert de Visée
(1660 - 1725)

Capriccio Op.100 No.11

[Group B]

Mauro Giuliani
(1781 - 1829)

11

Andantino Op.31 No.5

[Group B]

Fernando Sor
(1778 - 1839)

Etude in E Minor

[Group B]

Francisco Tárrega
(1852 - 1909)

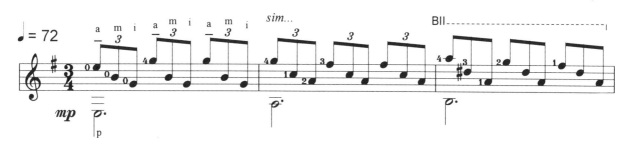

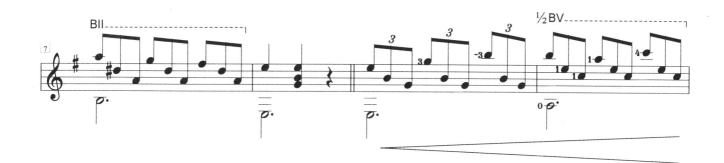

Allegretto

Manuel Ponce
(1886-1948)

[Group C]

Corsa

Reginald Smith Brindle
(1919 -)

[Group C]

16

Sea Prelude

Chaz Hart
(1948 -)

[Group C]

SECTION 3 – MUSICAL KNOWLEDGE

A maximum of 7 marks may be awarded in this section of the examination. The examiner will ask questions, based on the music performed, to test the candidate's knowledge of the rudiments of music, including diatonic intervals and principal modulations. The examiner will also expect an understanding of any terms and signs that appear in the music performed, and may ask basic questions about the composers. The information below provides a summary of what is required.

Rudiments

Candidates should have a good knowledge of basic musical rudiments, including an understanding of the value of notes and rests and the effect of dots and ties. The ability to identify and explain simple and compound time signatures is expected. Candidates should also be able to demonstrate an understanding of major and minor key signatures. Candidates lacking knowledge in this general area are advised to study for the L.C.M. Theory of Music examinations, using suitable music theory books, worksheets and musical dictionaries. Advice and tuition from an experienced teacher would undoubtedly prove helpful.

Intervals

Candidates will be expected to identify any diatonic interval, within the range of an octave, that occurs in the music performed. Candidates should always take note of the key signature before giving a response. Examples in the keys of C Major and C Minor are given below.

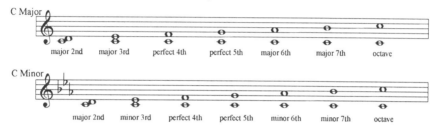

Modulations

Candidates should be able to identify any principal modulations that occur in the pieces performed. In particular, candidates should be able to recognise modulations to the dominant or sub-dominant, as well as to the relative major or minor.

Composers

For all the pieces performed, candidates should know the century in which the composer lived. Any supplementary questions will be very basic and relate only to the most well known composers such as John Dowland or Fernando Sor. No detailed knowledge will be expected at this grade.

Musical terms and signs

Candidates should have an understanding of any terms and signs, including dynamic markings, that appear in the music performed. Some examples are given below.

D.C. al Coda (Da Capo al Coda) – repeat from the beginning until the 'to Coda' marking.	*Fermata* (**) – sign indicating a pause.
D.S. al Fine (Dal Segno al Fine) – repeat from the sign (*) until the end (marked Fine).	*Allegretto* – fairly fast (not as fast as Allegro) *Andantino* – slightly slower or (normally) slightly faster than Andante (moderate 'walking' pace)
poco a poco – little by little.	*Capriccio* – normally a lively piece in light hearted style
sim (simile) – continue in a like manner .	*Rall (rallentando)* – becoming gradually slower.
più – more.	*Allargando* – getting slower and a little louder
pont. (Ponticello) – play near to the bridge.	*a tempo* – return to previous speed.
Ritmico – rhythmically.	*accel. (accelerando)* – gradually faster.
accent sign [>] – emphasise the note.	*Con moto* – with movement
tenuto sign [–] – hold the note for it's full value and slightly emphasise.	* ‰ ** ⌢

Candidates should also refer to the Introduction of this handbook which outlines the meaning of specialist guitar signs and symbols.

SECTION 4 – PLAYING AT SIGHT

The examiner will show you the sight reading test and allow you just a short time to look over it before performing it. A maximum of 10 marks may be awarded. The table below shows the range of the piece:

Length	Keys	Time signatures	Rhythms	Fingerboard positions
8 bars	Major: F, C, G, D Minor: D, A, E, B	2 3 4 6 4 4 4 8	o o. o o. ♩ ♪ ♪♪	1st / 2nd / 3rd

---

PERFORMANCE TIPS

1. Always check the key and time signature BEFORE you start to play.

2. Once you have identified the key it is helpful to remember that the notes will all come from the key scale – which you should already know from section one of this handbook, or from earlier grades.

3. Quickly scan through the piece and check any chords or rhythms that you are unsure of. Where fretted bass notes occur simultaneously with melody notes, decide which L/H fingering you will need to use.

4. Note the tempo or style marking, but be careful not to play at a tempo at which you cannot maintain accuracy throughout.

5. Once you start to play, try and keep your eyes on the music. Avoid the temptation to keep looking at the fingerboard – that's a sure way to lose your place in the music.

6. Observe all rests and try to follow the dynamic markings.

7. If you do make an error, try not to let it effect your confidence for the rest of the piece. It is more important to keep going and capture the overall shape of the piece, rather than keep stopping or going back to correct errors.

The examples below show the type of pieces that will be presented in the examination.

SECTION 5 - AURAL AWARENESS

A maximum of 8 marks may be awarded in this section of the examination. The tests will be played by the examiner on either guitar or piano, at the examiner's discretion. The examples below are shown in guitar notation and give a broad indication of the type of tests that will be given during the examination. Candidates wishing to view the piano notation for these tests should obtain the London College Of Music *Sample Ear Tests* booklet.

Rhythm tests

1. The examiner will twice play a short piece of music in 2, 3, 4 or 6/8 time, similar to the examples below. During the second playing, the candidate should beat time with a clear beat, in time with the examiner's playing. The examiner will take the response only from the beat, and will not accept a verbal description of the time signature. *(To beat time, begin with your arm out in front of you, with your hand at eye level. The first beat of each bar should be shown by a strong downwards motion of the arm. In 3 time, move the arm to the right for beat two and return to the top of your "triangle" for beat three. 4 time will involve a horizontal move to the left for beat two and to the right for beat three; the final fourth beat being a return upwards to your starting position. If you are left-handed, you should swap the left and right motions. 6/8 time should be beat as two dotted crotchet beats – one down and one up).*

2. The examiner will play one phrase of the piece again in a single line version. The candidate should reproduce the rhythm of this phrase by tapping or clapping. Tests will contain notes no shorter than a semiquaver. Simple dotted patterns may be included. The example below is taken from the second piece, bars 2 to 4.

Pitch tests
1. The examiner will play a key chord followed by a major or minor diatonic interval within the range of one octave. The candidate should identify the interval.

major 7th   *minor 3rd*   *major 6th*   *minor 2nd*

2. The examiner will show the candidate three similar versions of a short tune. One version will be played to the candidate twice. The candidate must state which version was played. Two examples are shown below.

22